Name ______________________ Class ______________ Date ______________

AF572598

Skills Worksheet

Directed Reading

Lesson: Safety Around Home

1. What is an accident?

____

____

FALLS

2. List four things you can do to prevent falls.

____

____

____

____

FIRES

3. A ______________________ is a small, battery-operated alarm that detects smoke from a fire.

4. A ______________________ is a device that releases chemicals to put out a fire.

ELECTROCUTION

5. What is electrocution?

____

____

CYCLING AND SKATING SAFETY

6. List five things you can do to stay safe while you cycle or skate.

____

____

____

____

____

VEHICLE SAFETY

______ **7.** Which of the following is the leading cause of injury and death for children and teens?
a. drowning
b. vehicle accidents
c. fires
d. falls

Lesson: Safety at School

8. Define *violence.*

____

____

VIOLENCE

______ **9.** Which of the following can lead to violence at school?
a. anger
b. illegal drugs
c. prejudice
d. All of the above

STAYING SAFE

10. Name four ways you can avoid violence.

____

____

____

____

Lesson: Seven Ways to Protect Yourself

THINK BEFORE YOU ACT

11. Why is it important to think before you act?

____

____

____

PAY ATTENTION

12. How does paying attention keep you safe?

____

____

KNOW YOUR LIMITS

13. Describe how knowing your limits can keep you safe.

____

____

PRACTICE REFUSAL SKILLS

14. How can you practice refusal skills?

____

____

USE SAFETY EQUIPMENT

15. How can safety equipment help you if you have an accident?

____

____

CHANGE RISKY BEHAVIOR

16. List two examples of risky behavior.

____

____

CHANGE RISKY SITUATIONS

17. What should you do if you see a risky situation?

____

____

Lesson: Safety in the Water

18. A ______________________ is a vest that keeps you floating in the water.

BOATING SAFELY

19. List four things you can do to make boating safe.

____

____

____

____

SWIMMING SAFELY

20. List seven ways to stay safe while swimming.

____

____

____

____

____

____

____

DIVING SAFELY

21. What could happen if you dive into shallow water?

____

____

AVOID DROWNING

22. Name three things that increase your chance of drowning.

____

____

____

SAVING A DROWNING PERSON

23. Describe how to save a drowning person.

____

____

____

____

WATER SURVIVAL

24. You can use the ______________________ if you get too tired when you are swimming.

Lesson: Weather Emergencies and Natural Disasters

25. A ______________________ is a natural event that causes widespread injury, death, and property damage.

RECOGNIZING WEATHER EMERGENCIES

26. What system warns people about weather emergencies?

____

THUNDERSTORMS

27. Describe a thunderstorm.

____

____

TORNADOES

28. What is a tornado?

____

____

29. A ______________________ is a weather alert that lets people know that a tornado may happen. A ______________________ is a weather alert that lets people know that a tornado has been spotted.

HURRICANES

30. Describe a hurricane.

____

____

FLOODS

31. A ______________________ is a flood that rises and falls with very little warning.

EARTHQUAKES

32. Name three possible effects of earthquakes.

____

____

____

Lesson: Dealing with Emergencies

WHEN TO GIVE FIRST AID

33. Why should you give first aid only if you have taken a first-aid class?

____

____

MAKING EMERGENCY PHONE CALLS

34. In case of an emergency, dial ______________________.

Lesson: Giving First Aid

35. An ______________________ is the process of applying pressure to a choking person's stomach to force an object out of their throat.

GIVING ABDOMINAL THRUSTS

36. How do you know if someone is choking?

____

____

GIVING RESCUE BREATHING

37. An emergency technique in which a rescuer gives air to someone who is not breathing is called ______________________.

CARING FOR VICTIMS OF POISONING

38. Name three things around your home that could cause poisoning.

____

____

____

TREATING WOUNDS

39. What should you wear when you help someone treat a cut?

____

TREATING BURNS

40. List and describe the three types of burns.

____

____

____

____

____

____

Name ______________________ Class ______________ Date ____________

Skills Worksheet

Concept Mapping

Lesson: Safety Around Home

Use the following terms to complete the concept map below: *electrocution, accidents, smoke detectors, fire extinguishers,* and *falls.*

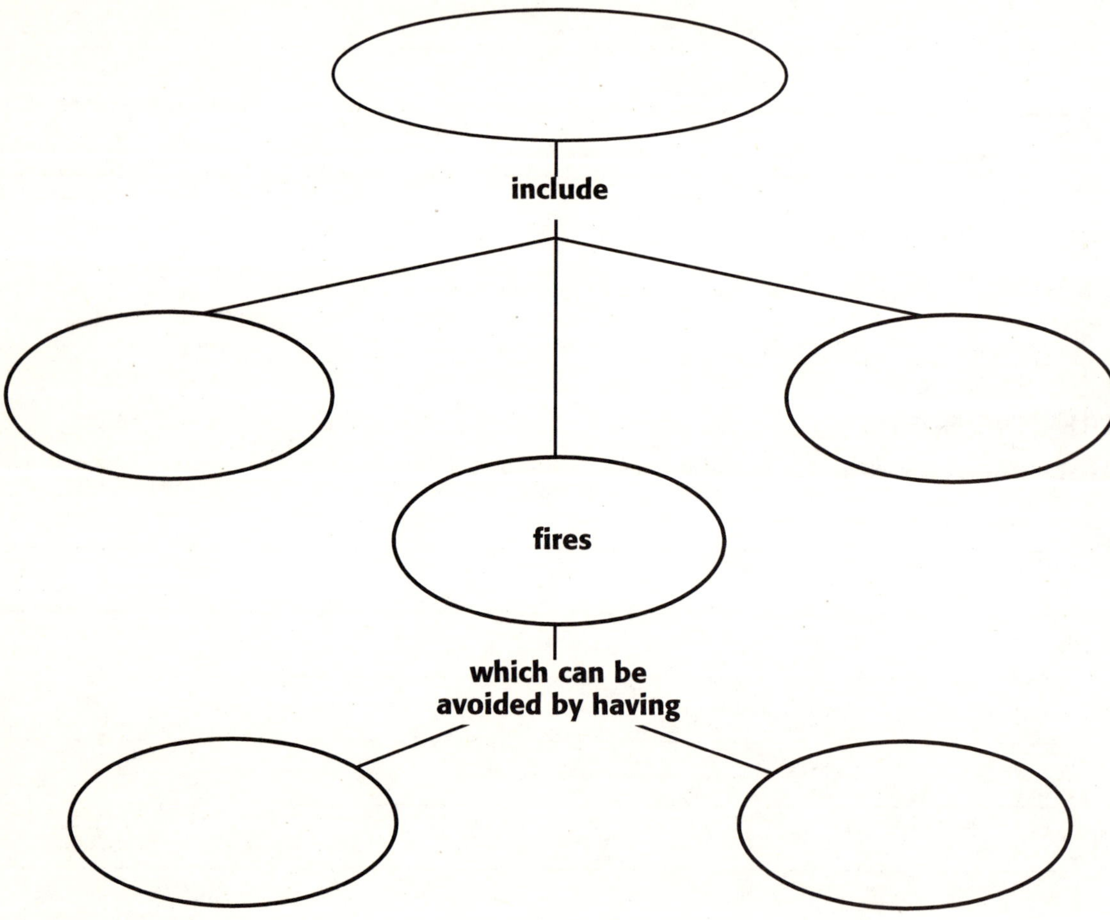

Name ______________________ Class ______________ Date ____________

Skills Worksheet

Concept Mapping

Lesson: Weather Emergencies and Natural Disasters

Use the following terms to create a concept map below: *warnings, earthquakes, natural disasters, floods, Emergency Alert System, thunderstorms, hurricanes, watches,* and *tornadoes.*

Name ________________ Class ________ Date ________

Skills Worksheet

Concept Review

Lesson: Safety Around Home

1. Describe three accidents that happen at home.

____

____

____

______ 2. Which of the following is NOT a way to stay safe in a vehicle?
   a. Wear your seat belt.
   b. Put young children in a safety seat.
   c. Put children younger than 12 in the back seat.
   d. Distract the driver.

3. Describe five ways to stay safe when you cycle or skate.

____

____

____

____

____

4. A ______________ is an alarm that detects smoke from a fire.

5. A ______________ releases chemicals to put out a fire.

Lesson: Safety at School

6. List five causes of violence.

____

____

____

7. Using physical force to hurt someone or cause damage is called

______________.

8. A ______________ is a group of people who often use violence.

9. List four ways to avoid violence in school.

Lesson: Seven Ways to Protect Yourself

10. List the seven safety rules and describe how they can protect you from accidental injury.

Lesson: Safety in the Water

11. Explain why you should wear a life jacket while boating.

12. List seven ways to stay safe while swimming.

Name ______________________ Class ______________ Date ____________

Write the letter of the correct answer in the space provided.

______ **13.** Which of the following is NOT a good way to avoid drowning?
- **a.** swimming alone
- **b.** obeying warning signs
- **c.** wearing a life jacket
- **d.** swimming near a lifeguard

______ **14.** Which is NOT a good way to save a drowning person?
- **a.** call for help
- **b.** jump into the water
- **c.** throw a life preserver
- **d.** All of the above

15. How should you get into an unfamiliar body of water?

____

____

16. What technique can you use if you are too tired to keep swimming?

____

____

Lesson: Weather Emergencies and Natural Disasters

Match each item in the right column to the correct term in the left column. Write the letter in the space provided.

______ **17.** overflowing of water into areas that are normally dry

______ **18.** spinning column of air that has high wind speeds and touches the ground

______ **19.** large, spinning tropical weather system that has wind speeds of at least 74 miles per hour

______ **20.** natural event that causes widespread injury, death, and property damage

______ **21.** shaking of the Earth's surface caused by movement along a break in the Earth's crust

______ **22.** heavy rainstorm with strong winds, lightning, and thunder

- **a.** natural disaster
- **b.** thunderstorm
- **c.** tornado
- **d.** hurricane
- **e.** flood
- **f.** earthquake

23. List three ways to learn about weather emergencies.

____

____

____

Lesson: Dealing with Emergencies

24. Emergency medical care for someone who has been hurt or who is sick is called ______________________.

25. Describe when you should give first aid.

____

____

____

26. List five things you should tell an operator during an emergency phone call.

____

____

____

____

____

Lesson: Giving First Aid

27. Explain how to give abdominal thrusts to an adult.

____

____

____

____

____

____

28. An emergency technique in which a rescuer gives air to someone who is not breathing is called ________________________.

29. Describe how to treat a victim of poisoning.

30. Describe how to treat wounds.

31. List and describe the three types of burns.

Name ______________________ Class ______________ Date ____________

Assessment

Refusal Skills

Lesson: Safety at School

Imagine that you are the advice columnist for the school newspaper. Read the letter below. Then write a response that uses refusal skills to help the writer of the letter.

Dear Know-It-All,

There is a boy in my class who carries a knife to school. He keeps it in his backpack. He keeps pressuring me to look at the knife after school, and then scare some other kids with it. I don't know what to do. Should I tell someone? I don't want to get him into trouble, but it makes me a little nervous.

Sincerely,

Scared

Name ______________________ Class ______________ Date ____________

Skills Worksheet

Refusal Skills

Lesson: Seven Ways to Protect Yourself

Describe how you would use the following refusal skills to respond to the following scenario. Remember to be clear and choose your words carefully. Describe your body language as well as your words.

You and some friends are fishing on the banks of a river. It's a hot day and your friends decide they want to jump in to cool off. Your parents have warned you that rivers can have dangerous currents. Even if you're a good swimmer, you can drown. Your friends keep pressuring you, and the river looks very inviting.

1. **Say no.** How would you tell your friends no?

____

____

2. **Offer an alternative.** What could you do instead of jumping into the river?

____

____

3. **Stand your ground.** What would you do if your friends kept pressuring you to jump in?

____

____

4. **Walk away.** Describe how you would get out of the situation.

____

____

5. **Plan ahead.** What could you do to avoid this situation?

____

____

____

6. **Have a support system.** Who will stand by you when you are in this situation? How can you use these people as support when dealing with this situation?

____

____

____

Name ______________________ Class ______________ Date ______________

Skills Worksheet

Decision-Making Skills

Lesson: Safety in the Water

Read the following situation. Then, follow the steps below to decide what you would do in this situation.

You and your friend Marcus are swimming in the deep end of the pool. You are having a lot of fun jumping off the side of the pool. Then suddenly, Marcus jumps in but is too tired to keep swimming. He is yelling for help. You look around and can't find a lifeguard.

1. **Identify the problem.** What decision do you have to make?

____

____

2. **Consider your values.** What is important to you?

____

____

3. **List the options.** What possible actions could you take?

____

____

4. **Weigh the consequences.** List the pros and cons of each option.

____

____

5. **Decide and act.** Describe what you will do. Explain your decision.

____

____

____

6. **Evaluate your choice.** How do you feel about the action you took? Did you make a good decision? Would you take a different action if faced with the same scenario again?

____

____

____

Name ______________________ Class ______________ Date ____________

Skills Worksheet

Decision-Making Skills

Lesson: Dealing with Emergencies

Read the following story and then write an ending to the story in the space below. Remember to include some of the decision-making skills you have learned.

Bethany was babysitting her little brother, Timmy, while their parents were at the store. Bethany was pushing Timmy on the swing in the backyard. Suddenly, Timmy fell off the swing. Bethany ran over to Timmy and noticed he was unconscious. She tried yelling his name, but he didn't respond.

Name ______________________ Class ______________ Date ____________

Skills Worksheet

Cross-Disciplinary: Language Arts

Lesson: Weather Emergencies and Natural Disasters

Write a short play about a weather emergency. Write about a thunderstorm, tornado, hurricane, flood, or earthquake. Include at least three characters. Describe the weather emergency and how the characters find safety.

Name ______________________ Class ______________ Date ____________

Skills Worksheet

Cross-Disciplinary: Art

Lesson: Giving First Aid

Make a poster that demonstrates rescue breathing. Draw a picture to illustrate each step. Include a description of each step under the picture. Your poster should be clear and easy to follow during an emergency situation. Use the space below to sketch some ideas for your poster. Then, use a computer graphics program to create the poster.

Name ______________________ Class ______________ Date ____________

Assessment

Quiz

Lesson: Safety Around Home

Write the letter of the correct answer in the space provided.

______ **1.** Which of the following is a type of accident that can occur around home?
a. electrocution
b. fall
c. fire
d. All of the above

______ **2.** How can you prevent falls?
a. Leave objects on the stairs.
b. Use a chair to get items that are out of reach.
c. Wipe up spills right away.
d. All of the above

______ **3.** What can you use to detect smoke from a fire?
a. fire extinguisher
b. smoke detector
c. Emergency Alert System
d. None of the above

______ **4.** What can you use to put out a fire?
a. fire extinguisher
b. smoke detector
c. Emergency Alert System
d. None of the above

______ **5.** How can you avoid electrocution?
a. Touch bare electrical wires.
b. Avoid putting too many plugs in an outlet.
c. Do not put safety covers on outlets.
d. Use the blow-dryer in the bathtub.

______ **6.** How can you stay safe in a vehicle?
a. Distract the driver.
b. Lay down in the back seat.
c. Wear your seat belt.
d. None of the above

Name ______________________________ Class ______________ Date ____________

Assessment

Quiz

Lesson: Safety at School

Match the definitions with the correct term. Write the letter in the space provided.

______ **1.** forming an opinion about other people because they are different

______ **2.** using physical force to hurt someone or cause damage

______ **3.** group of people who often use violence

a. violence

b. gang

c. prejudice

Write the letter of the correct answer in the space provided.

______ **4.** Which of the following is a cause of violence at school?

a. stress

b. illegal drugs

c. negative peer pressure

d. All of the above

______ **5.** If you overhear someone at school threatening violence, what should you NOT do?

a. keep it to yourself

b. tell a parent

c. tell a school counselor

d. All of the above

Name ______________________ Class ______________ Date ____________

Assessment

Quiz

Lesson: Seven Ways to Protect Yourself

Write the letter of the correct answer in the space provided.

______ **1.** Which of the following is NOT a good way to protect yourself?
- **a.** think before you act
- **b.** ignore your surroundings
- **c.** know your limits
- **d.** use safety equipment

______ **2.** Which of the following is an example of safety equipment?
- **a.** helmet
- **b.** rubber gloves
- **c.** goggles
- **d.** All of the above

______ **3.** Which of the following is a risky behavior?
- **a.** not wearing your seat belt
- **b.** wearing a helmet while cycling
- **c.** closing cabinet doors
- **d.** None of the above

______ **4.** What safety equipment should you wear when you go skating?
- **a.** helmet
- **b.** elbow pads
- **c.** knee pads
- **d.** All of the above

______ **5.** What should you do if someone you know has a risky behavior?
- **a.** ignore it
- **b.** talk to him or her about it
- **c.** try the risky behavior yourself
- **d.** None of the above

______ **6.** What should you do if you spot a risky situation?
- **a.** ignore it
- **b.** tell an adult
- **c.** fix it, even if you get hurt
- **d.** All of the above

Name ______________________ Class ______________ Date ____________

Assessment

Quiz

Lesson: Safety in the Water

Write the letter of the correct answer in the space provided.

______ **1.** How should you get into an unfamiliar body of water?
- **a.** dive head first
- **b.** lower yourself in feet first
- **c.** jump into the water
- **d.** None of the above

______ **2.** Which of the following is NOT a safe boating practice?
- **a.** standing in the boat
- **b.** going with an experienced person
- **c.** avoiding bad weather
- **d.** All of the above

______ **3.** Which of the following will keep you safe while swimming?
- **a.** Don't swim alone.
- **b.** Swim in designated areas.
- **c.** Watch out for boats.
- **d.** All of the above

______ **4.** What should you do to avoid drowning?
- **a.** swim alone
- **b.** horseplay
- **c.** swim in areas with a lifeguard on duty
- **d.** None of the above

______ **5.** What should you NOT do to help a person who is drowning?
- **a.** jump into the water
- **b.** throw a life preserver
- **c.** call for help
- **d.** All of the above

______ **6.** What should you do if you get tired while swimming?
- **a.** don't panic
- **b.** use the water survival float
- **c.** yell and wave for help
- **d.** All of the above

Name ______________________ Class ______________ Date ____________

Assessment

Quiz

Lesson: Weather Emergencies and Natural Disasters

Match the definitions with the correct term. Write the letter in the space provided.

______ **1.** shaking of the Earth's surface caused by movement along a break in the Earth's crust

______ **2.** system used by radio and TV stations to warn people of a weather emergency

______ **3.** natural event that causes widespread injury, death, and property damage

______ **4.** spinning column of air that has high wind speed and touches the ground

______ **5.** large, spinning tropical weather system that has wind speeds of at least 74 miles per hour

______ **6.** overflowing of water into areas that are normally dry

______ **7.** heavy rainstorm with strong winds, lightning, and thunder

______ **8.** water that rises and falls with little warning; caused by very heavy rainfall in a short amount of time

______ **9.** weather alert that lets people know a tornado has been spotted

______ **10.** weather alert that lets people know that a tornado may happen

a. natural disaster
b. thunderstorm
c. tornado
d. hurricane
e. flood
f. earthquake
g. EAS
h. flash flood
i. watch
j. warning

Name ______________________ Class ______________ Date ____________

Assessment

Quiz

Lesson: Dealing with Emergencies

Write the letter of the correct answer in the space provided.

______ **1.** When should you give first aid?
- **a.** when someone is unconscious
- **b.** when someone is not breathing
- **c.** when you have taken a first-aid class
- **d.** All of the above

______ **2.** When should you NOT give first aid?
- **a.** when someone is not breathing
- **b.** when someone is in pain
- **c.** if you are in danger
- **d.** All of the above

______ **3.** What information should you give the operator during an emergency phone call?
- **a.** your name
- **b.** your location
- **c.** the type of emergency
- **d.** All of the above

______ **4.** What should you NOT do during an emergency call?
- **a.** hang up right away
- **b.** tell the operator what you have done to treat the victim
- **c.** give your location
- **d.** All of the above

______ **5.** If you see a house on fire, what should you do?
- **a.** run inside to see if someone needs help
- **b.** call 911
- **c.** ignore it
- **d.** None of the above

Name ______________________ Class ______________ Date ____________

Assessment

Quiz

Lesson: Giving First Aid

Write the letter of the correct answer in the space provided.

______ **1.** What technique should you use to help a person who is choking?
- **a.** abdominal thrusts
- **b.** water survival float
- **c.** rescue breathing
- **d.** None of the above

______ **2.** What technique should you use if a person is not breathing?
- **a.** abdominal thrusts
- **b.** water survival float
- **c.** rescue breathing
- **d.** None of the above

______ **3.** Which of the following is the most serious type of burn?
- **a.** first-degree
- **b.** sunburn
- **c.** second-degree
- **d.** third-degree

______ **4.** How should you treat a first-degree burn?
- **a.** run cool water over the burn
- **b.** pour ice water over the burn
- **c.** call an ambulance
- **d.** All of the above

______ **5.** What household items can cause poisoning?
- **a.** pesticides
- **b.** cleaning products
- **c.** car fluids
- **d.** All of the above

Name ______________________ Class ______________ Date ____________

Assessment

Chapter Test

Health and Your Safety

USING VOCABULARY

Use the terms from the following list to complete each sentence below. A term may be used only once. Some terms will not be used.

accident	smoke detector	fire extinguisher
violence	gang	lifejacket
tornado	flood	rescue breathing
first aid	abdominal thrust	

1. A ______________________ is a small, battery-operated alarm that detects smoke from a fire.

2. Using physical force to hurt someone or cause damage is called ______________________.

3. Emergency medical care for someone who has been hurt or is sick is called ______________________.

4. An emergency technique in which a rescuer gives air to someone who is not breathing is called ______________________.

5. A ______________________ is a spinning column of air that has high wind speeds and touches the ground.

6. A ______________________ is a vest that keeps you floating in the water.

UNDERSTANDING CONCEPTS

Write the letter of the correct answer in the space provided.

______ **7.** What is the leading cause of death for children and teens?

a. electrocution
b. drowning
c. vehicle accidents
d. falls

______ **8.** During which type of natural disaster does the ground shake?

a. thunderstorm
b. earthquake
c. hurricane
d. flood

______ **9.** A large, spinning tropical weather system that has wind speeds of at least 74 miles per hour is called a(n)

a. thunderstorm.
b. earthquake.
c. hurricane.
d. flood.

_______**10.** An overflowing of water into areas that are normally dry is called a(n)

a. thunderstorm.
c. hurricane.
b. earthquake.
d. flood.

_______**11.** A heavy rainstorm with strong winds, lightning and thunder is called a(n)

a. thunderstorm.
c. hurricane.
b. earthquake.
d. flood.

_______**12.** Which of the following causes of violence means forming an opinion about other people because they are different?

a. stress
c. anger
b. prejudice
d. negative peer pressure

_______**13.** Which is the least severe type of burn?

a. first-degree
c. second-degree
b. third-degree
d. chemical

_______**14.** What technique is used to help someone who is choking?

a. rescue breathing
c. water survival float
b. EAS
d. abdominal thrusts

15. Explain what happens when someone is electrocuted.

____

____

____

____

____

16. Describe five causes of violence.

____

____

____

____

____

____

____

17. List seven ways to protect yourself from accidental injury.

____

____

____

____

____

____

____

18. List five tips for boating safely.

____

____

____

____

____

19. Explain how to treat a third-degree burn.

____

____

CRITICAL THINKING

20. Steve walked into his kitchen. The sink was full of water, and the electric can opener was sitting next to the sink. The can opener, microwave, toaster, blender, and mixer are all plugged into the same outlet. There is some juice spilled on the floor. Help Steve identify the potential accidents in the kitchen. Then, identify how to fix these risky situations.

____

____

____

____

____

____

21. How can first aid influence the chances of making a full recovery from an accident or an injury?

____

____

INTERPRETING GRAPHICS

Examine the diagram below, and answer the questions that follow.

Caring for Burns

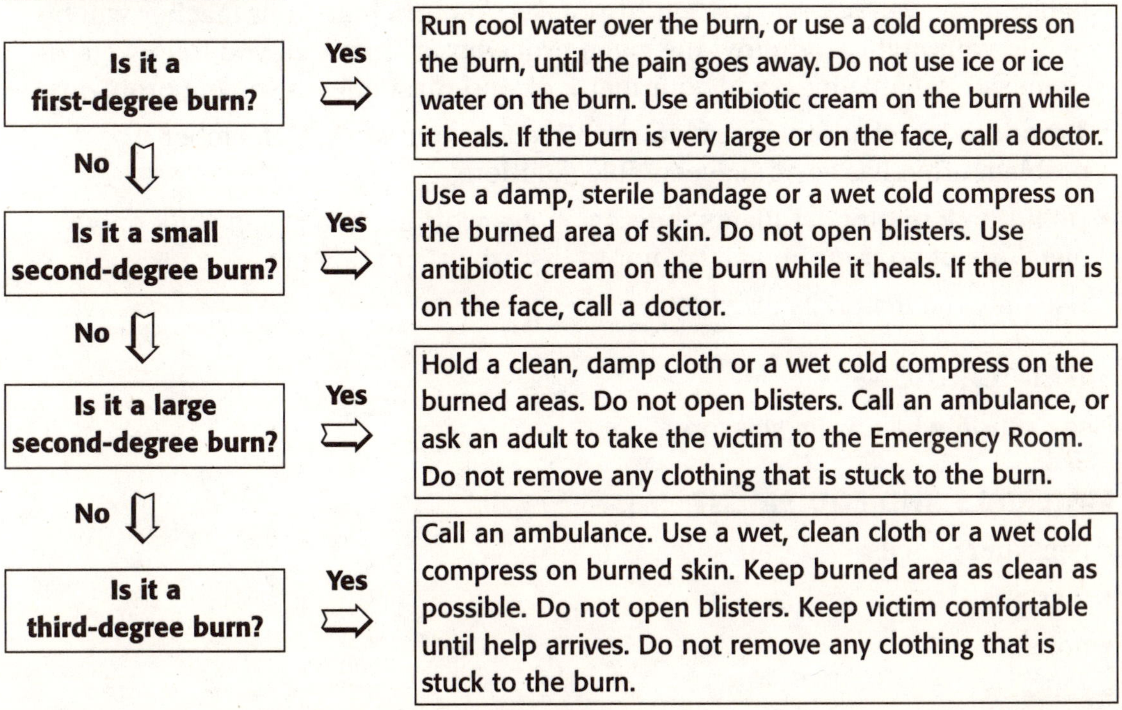

Is it a first-degree burn?	**Yes** ⇨	Run cool water over the burn, or use a cold compress on the burn, until the pain goes away. Do not use ice or ice water on the burn. Use antibiotic cream on the burn while it heals. If the burn is very large or on the face, call a doctor.
No ⇩		
Is it a small second-degree burn?	**Yes** ⇨	Use a damp, sterile bandage or a wet cold compress on the burned area of skin. Do not open blisters. Use antibiotic cream on the burn while it heals. If the burn is on the face, call a doctor.
No ⇩		
Is it a large second-degree burn?	**Yes** ⇨	Hold a clean, damp cloth or a wet cold compress on the burned areas. Do not open blisters. Call an ambulance, or ask an adult to take the victim to the Emergency Room. Do not remove any clothing that is stuck to the burn.
No ⇩		
Is it a third-degree burn?	**Yes** ⇨	Call an ambulance. Use a wet, clean cloth or a wet cold compress on burned skin. Keep burned area as clean as possible. Do not open blisters. Keep victim comfortable until help arrives. Do not remove any clothing that is stuck to the burn.

22. Explain how you would treat a small second-degree burn differently than you would treat a first-degree burn.

____

____

____

23. Explain how you would treat a third-degree burn differently than you would treat a large second-degree burn.

____

____

____

Name ______________________ Class ____________ Date ____________

Assessment

Performance-Based Assessment

A Classroom Emergency Action Plan

INTRODUCTION

You've read about what to do in emergency situations. Now you will have a chance to make an emergency action plan for the classroom.

OBJECTIVE

- Keep in mind that your teacher will be observing and grading your in-class behavior as well as your written responses. In particular, your teacher will be noting your ability to follow the given procedures, how well you follow classroom safety guidelines, and your methods and reasoning in solving problems.
- Try not to let what others are doing influence your work. Remember that a problem often has several acceptable solutions.
- Do not talk to other students unless you are working in a group. Talk only to members of your group and try not to disturb other students.
- Use only the materials provided.

SAFETY CAUTIONS

Use caution when using scissors.

MATERIALS AND EQUIPMENT

- pens and pencils
- markers
- notepads
- scissors
- poster board

PROCEDURE

1. Work with 1 or 2 other students. Choose a type of weather emergency.
2. Write an emergency action plan for your class to follow if the weather emergency you chose were to occur. Include information such as where to go and what to do.
3. Based on the plan you have written, make a poster that shows the steps your classmates should follow in case of an emergency. Use pictures and diagrams and make the poster clear and easy to read in an emergency situation.
4. Present your action plan to the class.

ANALYSIS

Answer the following questions in the space provided. Support your answers by explaining your reasoning.

5. What was the most common weather emergency chosen? Why do think that was?

____

____

____

____

____

6. If there was an earthquake while you were sitting at your desk, what could you do?

____

____

____

____

____

7. Why is it important to have an emergency action plan?

____

____

____

____

____

8. Who would you turn to for instructions during a weather emergency at school?

____

____

____

____

____

Name ______________________ Class ______________ Date ____________

Activity

Datasheet for In-Text Activity

Accidents at Home

1. In groups, write down five accidents that happened in your home last week. How often did each happen?
2. Make a bar graph of your results. The graph should show the kinds of accidents and how often they happen.

ANALYSIS

1. Which type of accident is the most common? Which type is the least common?

____

____

2. What can you do to prevent the accidents you listed from happening?

____

____

____

Name ______________________ Class ______________ Date ____________

Activity

Life Skills: Assessing Your Health

Lesson: Safety Around Home

CHECKING SMOKE DETECTORS AT HOME

Do a smoke detector check of your home. Check to make sure all of your smoke detectors have good batteries and are working properly.

1. How many rooms are in your home?

____

2. How many smoke detectors are in your home?

____

3. How many smoke detectors should you have in your home?

____

4. How can a smoke detector help you in case of a fire?

____

____

____

____

____

5. Why is it important to have a smoke detector in every room of your home?

____

____

____

____

____

6. How often should you check your smoke detectors to make sure they are working properly?

____

____

____

____

Name ______________________ Class ____________ Date ____________

Activity

Life Skills: Coping

Lesson: Dealing with Emergencies

HANDLING AN EMERGENCY AT HOME

Imagine that you are at home alone when the smoke detector goes off. You notice smoke coming from the upstairs area of your home.

1. What should you do first?

____

____

2. Where could you go to call for help?

____

____

3. What number should you dial to get help?

____

4. What information should you give the operator when you make the emergency phone call?

____

____

____

5. When should you hang up the phone?

____

____

6. What would you do if someone else was in the house with you?

____

____

____

Name ______________________ Class ______________ Date ____________

Activity

Enrichment Activity

Lesson: Safety Around Home

Interview a firefighter about fire safety at home. You may want to ask the following questions:

- About how many fires per month do you respond to?
- What are the most common causes of household fires?
- Do most people who escape from fires uninjured have smoke detectors?
- What should you do if there is a fire at home?
- What suggestions do you have to help people prevent fires?

Write at least three paragraphs to summarize the interview.

Lesson: Safety at School

Survey at least 30 other students about violence at your school. Ask each student the following question:

- What is the most common cause of violence at school?

1. What was the most common response?

____

____

____

2. What was the least common response?

____

____

____

Make a bar graph of your results

Lesson: Seven Ways to Protect Yourself

Survey 25 other students about their use of safety equipment. Find out how many people wear helmets while biking. Then find out how many people wear helmets, knee pads, and elbow pads while skating. Then, make two circle graphs showing the results of your survey. The first circle graph should show the percentages of people who do and do not wear helmets while biking. The second circle graph should show the percentages of people who do and do not wear helmets, knee pads, and elbow pads while skating.

Lesson: Safety in the Water

Create a magazine advertisement about boating safety. Include the following safety tips:

- Always wear a life jacket.
- Always go with an experienced person.
- Don't stand in a boat. The boat might tip over, or you might fall out.
- Avoid boating in bad weather.
- Avoid rough water unless you know how to handle it. If you're white-water rafting, wear a helmet to protect your head.

Your advertisement should include clear instructions and be easy to read and understand. Make it exciting by using photographs or drawings. Swap your advertisement with another student, and evaluate each other's advertisements for effectiveness.

Lesson: Weather Emergencies and Natural Disasters

Research the natural disasters that have occurred in your community during the past 100 years. Find out the number of each type of disaster that has occurred. Then, make a bar graph to present your findings. Your graph should show the kinds of disasters that have occurred and how many of each have occurred during the past 100 years.

Lesson: Dealing With Emergencies

Create an informational pamphlet to teach younger kids how to deal with emergencies. Your pamphlet should cover the following information:

- What first aid is
- When to give first aid
- Information about taking first-aid classes
- What to do if you are in danger
- How to make emergency phone calls

Include drawings in your pamphlet that demonstrate how to deal with emergencies.

Lesson: Giving First Aid

Produce a video that demonstrates how to give abdominal thrusts. Assume that the video will be used to teach younger students how to help people who are choking. Make sure your video covers the following topics:

- How to determine if someone is choking
- When to give abdominal thrusts
- The importance of calling for help
- How to give abdominal thrusts

Safety Caution: While making your demonstrational video, DO NOT actually give abdominal thrusts. Only pretend to give them in order to demonstrate. It is dangerous to give abdominal thrusts to someone who is not actually choking.

Name ________________ Class ________ Date ________

Activity

Health Inventory

Home Safety Checklist

Here is a questionnaire about home safety. Put a check next to each statement that applies to your home.

______ **1.** I leave objects on the stairs.

______ **2.** I leave objects lying on the floor.

______ **3.** I often forget to wipe up spills.

______ **4.** I stand on a chair to get to things I can't reach.

______ **5.** I often burn candles and forget to blow them out when I leave the room.

______ **6.** There are some frayed electrical cords lying around.

______ **7.** Power outlets are overloaded.

______ **8.** There is not a smoke detector in every room.

______ **9.** I'm not sure where the fire extinguisher is.

______ **10.** I keep my blow-dryer right next to the bathtub or sink.

______ **11.** Power outlets are uncovered.

______ **12.** Sometimes I forget to turn off the stove after I cook something.

Give yourself one point for each checkmark. Write your score here ______.

0–1: Your family is taking the precautions necessary to stay safe.

2–3: Overall, you family is taking safety precautions, but there is some room for improvement.

4–5: Your family could take steps to improve the safety of your home.

More than 5: You may have many dangerous situations in your home. Make a plan with your family to prevent potential accidents.

Name ______________________ Class ______________ Date ____________

Activity

Health Behavior Contract

Health and Your Safety

My Goals: I, ______________________________, will accomplish one or more of the following goals:

I will avoid violence.

I will make my house safer.

I will be safer around water.

Other: ______________________________

____

My Reasons: I can keep falls, fires, and electrocution from happening by paying attention, thinking before I act, knowing my limits, using refusal skills, using safety equipment, changing risky habits, and avoiding risky situations.

Other: ______________________________

____

My Values: Personal values that will help me meet my goals are

____

____

____

My Plan: The actions I will take to meet my goals are

____

____

____

Evaluation: I will use my Health Journal to keep a log of actions I took to fulfill this contract. After 1 month, I will evaluate my goals. I will adjust my plan if my goals are not being met. If my goals are being met, I will consider setting additional goals.

Signed ______________________________

Date ______________________________

Name ______________________ Class ______________ Date ____________

Activity

At-Home Activity

Fire Exit Plan

Work with a parent or caregiver to make a fire exit plan for your home. Follow the steps below.

1. Draw a diagram that shows all of the rooms in your home in the space below. You can use a separate sheet of paper if you need more space.

2. Mark all of the exits from your home in red.
3. Draw an arrow that shows the best exits from each room in case of a fire. Each room should have at least two exits.
4. Include a set of written instructions below the diagram that explains what to do in case of a fire.

The signatures below verify that our discussion has take place.

______________________________ ______________

Student Signature Class Period

______________________________ ______________

Parent or Guardian Signature Date

Name ______________________________ Class _______________ Date _____________

Activity

Actividad En Casa

Un plan de evacuación en caso de incendio

Trabaje con su padre/madre/tutor para elaborar un plan de evacuación en caso de incendio para su casa. Siga los pasos siguientes.

1. Dibuje un diagrama aquí que muestre todos los cuartos en su casa. Si necesita más espacio, use otra hoja de papel.

2. Marque en rojo todas las salidas de la casa.
3. Dibujen una flecha que muestre las mejores vías de evacuación de cada cuarto en caso de incendio. Cada cuarto debe tener un mínimo de dos salidas.
4. Incluya instrucciones escritas debajo del diagrama que expliquen los que se hace en caso de incendio.

Las firmas verifican que discutimos esta actividad juntos.

______________________________ ______________________________

Firma de Estudiante | Período de Clase(la Salud)

______________________________ ______________________________

Firma de Padre/Madre/Tutor | Fecha

Lesson Plan

Lesson: Safety Around Home

Pacing

45 minutes

Objectives

1. Describe three accidents that happen at home.
2. Describe five ways to stay safe when you cycle or skate.
3. List three ways to stay safe in a vehicle.

Standards Covered

1.1 (partial) Explain the relationship between positive health behaviors and the prevention of injury, illness, disease, and premature death.

3.1 Explain the importance of assuming responsibility for personal health behaviors.

3.4 Demonstrate strategies to improve or maintain personal and family health.

3.5 Develop injury prevention and management strategies for personal and family health.

KEY
SE = Student Edition **ATE** = Annotated Teacher Edition
CRF = Chapter Resource File

CHAPTER OPENER

- ❑ **Health IQ, SE** To assess student knowledge about health and safety, have students answer the Health IQ questions. Answers are at the bottom of the test.

FOCUS

- ❑ **Bellringer, ATE** Students list ways to avoid accidents around the home.
- ❑ **Bellringer Transparency** Use this transparency as students enter the classroom and find their seats.
- ❑ **Start Off Write, SE** Ask students to write an answer to the following question: "How can you stay safe while you are skating?"

MOTIVATE

- ❑ **Activity, Skit, ATE** Students write a skit about wearing bicycle helmets. **[General]**

TEACH

- ❑ **Hands-On Activity, Accidents at Home, SE** Students create a bar graph to show five accidents that happened in their home last week.
- ❑ **Datasheet for In-Text Activity, Accidents at Home, CRF** Students use this worksheet to record data for the Hands-On Activity.
- ❑ **Life Skills Activity, Practicing Wellness, SE** This activity asks students to draw pictures of accident risks around the home. **[GENERAL]**
- ❑ **Group Activity, School Fire Safety, ATE** This activity asks students to explore fire safety at school. **[GENERAL]**
- ❑ **Physical Science Connection, Electrocution and Lightning, ATE** This activity asks students to research lightning. **[ADVANCED]**
- ❑ **Life Skills: Assessing Your Health, CRF** This worksheet asks students to check the smoke detectors in their homes. **[GENERAL]**
- ❑ **Concept Mapping, CRF** This worksheet reviews the terms introduced in the lesson. **[GENERAL]**

CLOSE

- ❑ **Lesson Quiz, ATE** Students answer 4 questions about safety around home. **[GENERAL]**
- ❑ **Lesson Quiz, CRF** Students answer 6 questions about safety around home. **[GENERAL]**
- ❑ **Concept Review, CRF** This exercise reinforces the material covered in the lesson. **[GENERAL]**

HOMEWORK

- ❑ **Lesson Review, SE** Assign questions 1–6 for review, homework, or quiz.

OTHER RESOURCE OPTIONS

- ❑ **Internet Connect** Safety, HealthLinks Code HD4084. Students research Internet sources about safety.
- ❑ **go.hrw.com** For worksheets, videos, and other teaching aides related to this chapter, visit the HRW Web site and type in the keyword HD4SA6.
- ❑ **VideoSelect** Videos related to the chapter topics may be found at go.hrw.com. Type in the keyword HD4SA6V.
- ❑ **Guided Audio CD Program** Health and Your Safety. The audio program is a reading of the chapter content for ELL students, auditory learners, and struggling readers.
- ❑ **Enrichment Activity, CRF** Students interview a firefighter about fire safety at home. **[ADVANCED]**
- ❑ **Directed Reading, CRF** This worksheet guides students through the lesson content. **[BASIC]**

Lesson Plan

Lesson: Safety at School

Pacing

25 minutes

Objectives

1. List five causes of violence.
2. List four ways to avoid violence in school.

Standards Covered

1.1 (partial) Explain the relationship between positive health behaviors and the prevention of injury, illness, disease, and premature death.

3.4 Demonstrate strategies to improve or maintain personal and family health.

3.5 Develop injury prevention and management strategies for personal and family health.

3.6 Demonstrate ways to avoid and reduce threatening situations.

5.6 (partial) Demonstrate refusal and negotiation skills to enhance health.

5.7 (partial) Analyze the possible causes of conflict among youth in schools and communities.

KEY
SE = Student Edition **ATE** = Annotated Teacher Edition
CRF = Chapter Resource File

FOCUS

- ❑ **Bellringer, ATE** Students describe ways they handle their anger.
- ❑ **Bellringer Transparency** Use this transparency as students enter the classroom and find their seats.
- ❑ **Start Off Write, SE** Ask students to write an answer to the following question: "How can you avoid violence at school?"

MOTIVATE

- ❑ **Discussion, Stress Relief, ATE** Students discuss constructive ways to handle anger and stress. **[General]**

TEACH

- ❑ **Life Skills Activity, Using Refusal Skills, SE** This activity asks students to make a poster showing ways to use refusal skills to avoid violence in school.
- ❑ **Group Activity, Role-Playing, ATE** This activity asks students to practice avoiding violence and gangs. **[General]**

Lesson Plan *continued*

- ❑ **Refusal Skills, CRF** This worksheet helps students practice refusing to cover up a potentially violent situation at school. **[General]**

CLOSE

- ❑ **Lesson Quiz, ATE** Students answer 4 questions about violence. **[General]**
- ❑ **Lesson Quiz, CRF** Students answer 5 questions about tobacco violence. **[General]**
- ❑ **Concept Review, CRF** This exercise reinforces the material covered in the lesson. **[General]**

HOMEWORK

- ❑ **Lesson Review, SE** Assign questions 1–4 for review, homework, or quiz.
- ❑ **Enrichment Activity, CRF** Students survey thirty classmates about school violence and graph their results. **[Advanced]**

OTHER RESOURCE OPTIONS

- ❑ **go.hrw.com** For worksheets, videos, and other teaching aides related to this chapter, visit the HRW Web site and type in the keyword HD4SA6.
- ❑ **VideoSelect** Videos related to the chapter topics may be found at go.hrw.com. Type in the keyword HD4SA6V.
- ❑ **Guided Audio CD Program** Health and Your Safety. The audio program is a reading of the chapter content for ELL students, auditory learners, and struggling readers.
- ❑ **Directed Reading, CRF** This worksheet guides students through the lesson content. **[Basic]**

Lesson Plan

Lesson: Seven Ways to Protect Yourself

Pacing

20 minutes

Objectives

1. List seven ways to protect yourself from accidental injury.
2. Describe how the seven safety rules protect you from injury.

Standards Covered

1.1 (partial) Explain the relationship between positive health behaviors and the prevention of injury, illness, disease, and premature death.

3.1 Explain the importance of assuming responsibility for personal health behaviors.

3.4 Demonstrate strategies to improve or maintain personal and family health.

3.5 Develop injury prevention and management strategies for personal and family health.

5.6 (partial) Demonstrate refusal and negotiation skills to enhance health.

KEY
SE = Student Edition　　**ATE** = Annotated Teacher Edition
CRF = Chapter Resource File

FOCUS

- ❑ **Bellringer, ATE** Students write down five potentially dangerous situations in their classroom and then tell how they could protect themselves.
- ❑ **Bellringer Transparency** Use this transparency as students enter the classroom and find their seats.
- ❑ **Start Off Write, SE** Ask students to write an answer to the following question: "How does knowing your limits keep you safe?"

MOTIVATE

- ❑ **Activity, Mapping Danger, ATE** Students identify potentially dangerous spots in their neighborhoods. **[GENERAL]**

TEACH

- ❑ **Inclusion Strategies, ATE** Students practice assessing the safety of different situations. **[GENERAL]**
- ❑ **Discussion, Safety Equipment, ATE** This activity asks students to identify safety equipment used for different activities. **[GENERAL]**

- ❑ **Activity, Risky Behavior, ATE** This activity asks students to identify their own risky behaviors. **[BASIC]**
- ❑ **Refusal Skills, CRF** This worksheet helps students practice making good decisions about water safety. **[GENERAL]**

CLOSE

- ❑ **Lesson Quiz, ATE** Students answer 4 questions about safety and risky behaviors. **[GENERAL]**
- ❑ **Lesson Quiz, CRF** Students answer 6 questions about safety equipment and risky behviors. **[GENERAL]**
- ❑ **Concept Review, CRF** This exercise reinforces the material covered in the lesson. **[GENERAL]**

HOMEWORK

- ❑ **Lesson Review, SE** Assign questions 1–4 for review, homework, or quiz.
- ❑ **Enrichment Activity, CRF** Students survey twenty-five classmates about their use of safety equipment and then make two circle graphs to show the results. **[ADVANCED]**

OTHER RESOURCE OPTIONS

- ❑ **go.hrw.com** For worksheets, videos, and other teaching aides related to this chapter, visit the HRW Web site and type in the keyword HD4SA6.
- ❑ **VideoSelect** Videos related to the chapter topics may be found at go.hrw.com. Type in the keyword HD4SA6V.
- ❑ **Guided Audio CD Program** Health and Your Safety. The audio program is a reading of the chapter content for ELL students, auditory learners, and struggling readers.
- ❑ **Directed Reading, CRF** This worksheet guides students through the lesson content. **[BASIC]**

Lesson Plan

Lesson: Safety in the Water

Pacing

45 minutes

Objectives

1. Explain why you should wear a life jacket while boating.
2. List seven ways to stay safe while swimming.
3. Describe diving safety.
4. List four ways to avoid drowning.
5. Explain how you can rescue someone who is drowning.
6. Describe the water survival float.

Standards Covered

1.1 (partial) Explain the relationship between positive health behaviors and the prevention of injury, illness, disease, and premature death.

3.4 Demonstrate strategies to improve or maintain personal and family health.

3.5 Develop injury prevention and management strategies for personal and family health.

KEY
SE = Student Edition **ATE** = Annotated Teacher Edition
CRF = Chapter Resource File

FOCUS

- ❑ **Bellringer, ATE** Students discuss life jackets.
- ❑ **Bellringer Transparency** Use this transparency as students enter the classroom and find their seats.
- ❑ **Start Off Write, SE** Ask students to write an answer to the following question: "Why shouldn't you jump in the water to save someone who is drowning?"

MOTIVATE

- ❑ **Demonstration, Life Jackets, ATE** Students compare different flotation devices. **[General]**

Lesson Plan *continued*

TEACH

- ❑ **Life Skills Activity, Communicating Effectively, SE** This activity asks students to create a public service announcement that promotes safe swimming and diving.
- ❑ **Life Skill Builder, Coping, ATE** This activity asks students to discuss how they coped with a bad situation in the water. **[GENERAL]**
- ❑ **Discussion, The Buddy System, ATE** This worksheet asks students to discuss the buddy system. **[BASIC]**
- ❑ **Group Activity, Safety on the Water, ATE** This activity asks students to conduct an interview and create a poster on water safety. **[GENERAL]**
- ❑ **Inclusion Strategies, ATE** This activity asks students to practice the water survival float position. **[BASIC]**

CLOSE

- ❑ **Lesson Quiz, ATE** Students answer 4 questions about water safety. **[GENERAL]**
- ❑ **Lesson Quiz, CRF** Students answer 6 questions about water safety. **[GENERAL]**
- ❑ **Concept Review, CRF** This exercise reinforces the material covered in the lesson. **[GENERAL]**

HOMEWORK

- ❑ **Lesson Review, SE** Assign questions 1–7 for review, homework, or quiz.
- ❑ **Decision-Making Skills, CRF** Students must decide how to help a friend who could be drowning. **[GENERAL]**

OTHER RESOURCE OPTIONS

- ❑ **Internet Connect** Water Safety, HealthLinks Code HD4105. Students research Internet sources about water safety.
- ❑ **go.hrw.com** For worksheets, videos, and other teaching aides related to this chapter, visit the HRW Web site and type in the keyword HD4SA6.
- ❑ **VideoSelect** Videos related to the chapter topics may be found at go.hrw.com. Type in the keyword HD4SA6V.
- ❑ **Guided Audio CD Program** Health and Your Safety. The audio program is a reading of the chapter content for ELL students, auditory learners, and struggling readers.
- ❑ **Enrichment Activity, CRF** Students create a magazine advertisement about boating safety. **[ADVANCED]**
- ❑ **Directed Reading, CRF** This worksheet guides students through the lesson content. **[BASIC]**

Lesson Plan

Lesson: Weather Emergencies and Natural Disasters

Pacing

25 minutes

Objectives

1. List three ways to learn of weather emergencies.
2. Describe five events that can result in natural disasters.

Standards Covered

3.4 Demonstrate strategies to improve or maintain personal and family health.

3.5 Develop injury prevention and management strategies for personal and family health.

KEY	
SE = Student Edition	**ATE** = Annotated Teacher Edition
CRF = Chapter Resource File	

FOCUS

- ❑ **Bellringer, ATE** Students make a list of the types of natural disasters that affect their area.
- ❑ **Bellringer Transparency** Use this transparency as students enter the classroom and find their seats.
- ❑ **Start Off Write, SE** Ask students to write an answer to the following question: "Why shouldn't you take shelter under a tree during a thunderstorm?"

MOTIVATE

- ❑ **Discussion, Emergency Alert System, ATE** Students discuss the Emergency Alert System. **[General]**

TEACH

- ❑ **Debate, Storm Chasing, ATE** This activity asks students to research and debate whether storm chasing is a safe and effective way to study tornadoes. **[Advanced]**
- ❑ **Earth Science Connection, Making Models, ATE** This activity asks students to make a model of a tornado vortex. **[Basic]**
- ❑ **Group Activity, Flood Evacuation Plan, ATE** This activity asks students to create a flood evacuation plan. **[Advanced]**

CLOSE

- ❑ **Lesson Quiz, ATE** Students answer 4 questions about weather emergencies and natural disasters. **[GENERAL]**
- ❑ **Lesson Quiz, CRF** Students answer 10 questions about weather emergencies and natural disasters. **[GENERAL]**
- ❑ **Concept Review, CRF** This exercise reinforces the material covered in the lesson. **[GENERAL]**

HOMEWORK

- ❑ **Lesson Review, SE** Assign questions 1–4 for review, homework, or quiz.
- ❑ **Concept Mapping, CRF** Students use key concepts and vocabulary from the lesson to complete a concept map. **[GENERAL]**
- ❑ **Cross-Disciplinary: Language Arts, CRF** This worksheet asks students to write a play about finding safety during a weather emergency. **[GENERAL]**

OTHER RESOURCE OPTIONS

- ❑ **go.hrw.com** For worksheets, videos, and other teaching aides related to this chapter, visit the HRW Web site and type in the keyword HD4SA6.
- ❑ **VideoSelect** Videos related to the chapter topics may be found at go.hrw.com. Type in the keyword HD4SA6V.
- ❑ **Guided Audio CD Program** Health and Your Safety. The audio program is a reading of the chapter content for ELL students, auditory learners, and struggling readers.
- ❑ **Enrichment Activity, CRF** Students research natural disasters that have occurred in their community during the past 100 years. **[ADVANCED]**
- ❑ **Directed Reading, CRF** This worksheet guides students through the lesson content. **[BASIC]**

Lesson Plan

Lesson: Dealing with Emergencies

Pacing

20 minutes

Objectives

1. Describe when you should give first aid.
2. List five things you should tell an operator during an emergency phone call.

Standards Covered

1.1 (partial) Explain the relationship between positive health behaviors and the prevention of injury, illness, disease, and premature death.

2.6 Describe situations requiring professional health services.

KEY
SE = Student Edition **ATE** = Annotated Teacher Edition
CRF = Chapter Resource File

FOCUS

- ❑ **Bellringer, ATE** Students recall an accident or emergency in their home.
- ❑ **Bellringer Transparency** Use this transparency as students enter the classroom and find their seats.
- ❑ **Start Off Write, SE** Ask students to write an answer to the following question: "What information should you give during an emergency phone call?"

MOTIVATE

- ❑ **Group Activity, Poster Project, ATE** Students make a poster detailing some of the things to look for when a person gets hurt. **[GENERAL]**

TEACH

- ❑ **Life Skill Builder, Practicing Wellness, ATE** This activity asks students to describe ways of preparing for emergencies at home and at school. **[GENERAL]**
- ❑ **Life Skills: Coping, CRF** This worksheet asks students to discuss how they would respond to a fire in their home. **[GENERAL]**
- ❑ **Decision-Making Skills, CRF** This worksheet helps students practice making decisions in an emergency situation at home. **[GENERAL]**

Lesson Plan *continued*

CLOSE

- ❑ **Lesson Quiz, ATE** Students answer 3 questions about dealing with emergencies. [GENERAL]
- ❑ **Lesson Quiz, CRF** Students answer 5 questions about dealing with emergencies. [GENERAL]
- ❑ **Concept Review, CRF** This exercise reinforces the material covered in the lesson. [GENERAL]

HOMEWORK

- ❑ **Lesson Review, SE** Assign questions 1–3 for review, homework, or quiz.
- ❑ **Enrichment Activity, CRF** Students create an informational pamphlet to teach younger children how to deal with emergencies. [ADVANCED]

OTHER RESOURCE OPTIONS

- ❑ **go.hrw.com** For worksheets, videos, and other teaching aides related to this chapter, visit the HRW Web site and type in the keyword HD4SA6.
- ❑ **VideoSelect** Videos related to the chapter topics may be found at go.hrw.com. Type in the keyword HDSA6V.
- ❑ **Guided Audio CD Program** Health and Your Safety. The audio program is a reading of the chapter content for ELL students, auditory learners, and struggling readers.
- ❑ **Directed Reading, CRF** This worksheet guides students through the lesson content. [BASIC]

Lesson Plan

Lesson: Giving First Aid

Pacing

45 minutes

Objectives

1. Explain how to give abdominal thrusts to an adult.
2. Describe rescue breathing.
3. Describe how to treat a victim of poisoning.
4. Describe how to treat wounds.
5. Compare the three types of burns.

Standards Covered

1.1 (partial) Explain the relationship between positive health behaviors and the prevention of injury, illness, disease, and premature death.

2.6 Describe situations requiring professional health services.

KEY
SE = Student Edition **ATE** = Annotated Teacher Edition
CRF = Chapter Resource File

FOCUS

- ❑ **Bellringer, ATE** Students list poisonous household cleaning products.
- ❑ **Bellringer Transparency** Use this transparency as students enter the classroom and find their seats.
- ❑ **Start Off Write, SE** Ask students to write an answer to the following question: "How can you help someone who is choking?"

MOTIVATE

- ❑ **Discussion, Choking, ATE** Students discuss how to tell if a person is choking. **[BASIC]**

TEACH

- ❑ **Teaching Transparency, Rescue Breathing for Adults** Use this graphic to help students understand rescue breathing for adults.
- ❑ **Teaching Transparency, Caring for Burns** Use this graphic to help students understand how to care for burns.
- ❑ **Demonstration, Rescue Breathing, ATE** This activity demonstrates rescue breathing. **[BASIC]**

- ❑ **Life Skill Builder, Practicing Wellness, ATE** This activity asks students to write a magazine article about preventing the spread of blood-borne disease. **[General]**

CLOSE

- ❑ **Lesson Quiz, ATE** Students answer 3 questions about giving first aid. **[General]**
- ❑ **Lesson Quiz, CRF** Students answer 5 questions about giving first aid. **[General]**
- ❑ **Concept Review, CRF** This exercise reinforces the material covered in the lesson. **[General]**

HOMEWORK

- ❑ **Lesson Review, SE** Assign questions 1–5 for review, homework, or quiz.
- ❑ **Cross-Disciplinary: Art, CRF** This worksheet asks students to make a poster that demonstrates rescue breathing. **[General]**

OTHER RESOURCE OPTIONS

- ❑ **Internet Connect** First Aid, HealthLinks Code HD4042. Students research Internet sources about first aid.
- ❑ **go.hrw.com** For worksheets, videos, and other teaching aides related to this chapter, visit the HRW Web site and type in the keyword HD4SA6.
- ❑ **VideoSelect** Videos related to the chapter topics may be found at go.hrw.com. Type in the keyword HDSA6V.
- ❑ **Guided Audio CD Program** Health and Your Safety. The audio program is a reading of the chapter content for ELL students, auditory learners, and struggling readers.
- ❑ **Enrichment Activity, CRF** Students produce a video that demonstrates how to give abdominal thrusts. **[Advanced]**
- ❑ **Directed Reading, CRF** This worksheet guides students through the lesson content. **[Basic]**

Lesson Plan

End of Chapter Review and Assessment

Pacing

90 minutes

KEY
SE = Student Edition **ATE** = Annotated Teacher Edition
CRF = Chapter Resource File

REVIEW

- ❑ **Chapter Review, SE** Assign questions to review the material for this chapter. Use the assignment guide to customize review for lessons covered.
- ❑ **Concept Review, CRF** Vocabulary and concept review for each lesson. **[GENERAL]**

ASSESSMENT

- ❑ **Chapter Test, Health and Your Safety, CRF** Assign questions for general level chapter assessment. **[GENERAL]**

ALTERNATIVE ASSESSMENT

- ❑ **Alternative Assessment, Story Writing, ATE** Assign this activity for general level assessment for the lesson *Safety Around Home.* **[GENERAL]**
- ❑ **Alternative Assessment, Letter Writing, ATE** Assign this activity for general level assessment for the lesson *Safety at School.* **[GENERAL]**
- ❑ **Alternative Assessment, PSA, ATE** Assign this activity for general level assessment for the lesson *Seven Ways to Protect Yourself.* **[GENERAL]**
- ❑ **Alternative Assessment, Story Writing, ATE** Assign this activity for advanced level assessment for the lesson *Safety in the Water.* **[ADVANCED]**
- ❑ **Alternative Assessment, Flashcards, ATE** Assign this activity for general level assessment for the lesson *Giving First Aid.* **[GENERAL]**
- ❑ **Performance-Based Assessment, A Classroom Emergency Action Plan, CRF** Students create an emergency action plan for the classroom. **[GENERAL]**
- ❑ **Test Generator, One-Stop Planner** Create a customized homework, quiz, or test using the HRW Test Generator program.
- ❑ **Test Item Listing, CRF** Use the Test Item Listing to identify questions to use in a customized homework, quiz, or test.

Parent Letter

Health and Your Safety

Dear Parent/Guardian,

In the years to come, your child will be making decisions that impact his or her physical, emotional, and social health. The purpose of this Health Education class is to provide students with the knowledge and resources they need to make responsible and well-informed decisions about their health. As the course progresses, students will be asked to explore their values, opinions, and beliefs about health. It is important that students receive mature guidance in the classroom and at home as they address these issues.

In the next few weeks, your son or daughter's Health Education class will focus on the subject of health and safety. Your child's ability to make good decisions about safe behavior will influence not only how long he or she lives, but also the quality of his or her life. The chapter will introduce strategies for staying safe at home and at school.

Other topics covered in this chapter include water safety, weather emergencies, and natural disasters. We will also discuss dealing with emergencies and giving first aid.

You can actively support your son or daughter's progress in Health by communicating with him or her about the topics covered in this course. To aid this communication, I have included a worksheet called "Fire Exit Plan" for you to complete with your child. Your signature at the end of this material will verify that this home interaction has taken place.

Thank you in advance for your time, cooperation, and support.

Sincerely,

____

Health Teacher

Carta a los Padres/al Tutor

La salud y la seguridad

Estimado(s) Padres/Tutor:

En el futuro, su hijo/a va a hacer decisiones que influyan en su salud física, emocional y social. El motivo fundamental de la clase de Salud es proporcionarles a los estudiantes los conocimientos y recursos precisos para hacer responsables decisiones bien informadas en cuanto a su salud. Durante el año académico, los alumnos tendrán que revisar sus valores, opiniones y creencias sobre la salud. Es importante que, al confrontar estos asuntos, los jóvenes reciban informes y consejos de adultos tanto en el aula de clases como en casa.

En las próximas semanas, la clase de Salud se enfocará en el tema de la salud y la seguridad. La capacidad de hacer buenas decisiones sobre el comportamiento seguro va a influir tanto en cuántos años su hijo/a viva como en la calidad de su vida en el futuro. Este capítulo presentará estrategias para ser seguro/a en casa y en la escuela.

Otros asuntos tratados son la seguridad acuática, las emergencias del tiempo y los desastres naturales. También se discutirá las urgencias y las medidas de primer auxilio.

Ud. puede ayudar a su hijo/a en esta clase por hablar con él o ella sobre los temas que estudie. Para facilitar esta comunicación le mando una hoja de trabajo, *Un plan de evacuación en caso de incendio*, para completar con su hijo/a. Su firma en la hoja verifica que Uds. discutieron esta actividad juntos.

Gracias anticipadas por su tiempo, cooperación y apoyo.

Atentamente,

____

Maestro/a de Salud

Assessment

Performance-Based Assessment

A Classroom Emergency Action Plan

Teacher's Notes

INTRODUCTION

Students will make an emergency action plan for the classroom.

TIME REQUIRED One 45-minute class period

Students will need 25 minutes to create their plan, and 20 minutes to present their plans to the class.

PBA RATINGS

Easy ← 1 2 3 4 → Hard

Teacher Prep—1
Student Set-Up—2
Concept Level—1
Clean Up—2

ADVANCE PREPARATION

Obtain markers, scissors, and poster board for each student.

SAFETY CAUTIONS

Remind students to use caution when using scissors.

PERFORMANCE

At the end of the test, students should turn in the following items:

- Completed analysis questions from their workbook
- Completed action plan

EVALUATION

The following is a recommended breakdown for evaluating student performance:

30% Completion of plan

40% Understanding what to do in case of an emergency

30% Completed analysis questions

Answer Key

Directed Reading

LESSON: SAFETY AROUND HOME

1. An accident is an unexpected event that may lead to injury.
2. Don't leave objects on the stairs or floor. Use a ladder instead of a chair to get items that are out of reach. Wipe up spills right away. Watch for situations that could be hazardous for small children.
3. smoke detector
4. fire extinguisher
5. an accident in which electricity passes through the body
6. Pay attention to traffic, and avoid busy areas; follow the rules of the road; wear bright clothes, and don't ride or skate after dark; don't cycle or skate alone; always wear a helmet.
7. b

LESSON: SAFETY AT SCHOOL

8. Violence is using physical force to hurt someone or cause damage.
9. d
10. If you don't feel safe, talk to your parents or school counselor. If you know about a violent situation, tell an adult. Practice refusal skills and learn conflict management skills. Find a positive way to spend your time.

LESSON: SEVEN WAYS TO PROTECT YOURSELF

11. Thinking about the risks of your actions will help you avoid injuries.
12. It keeps you safe because you will know about accidents that could happen.
13. When you know your limits you will be less likely to get hurt and you will avoid risking something that is important to you.
14. Make up situations that are hard to refuse. Practice different ways to say no with parents or friends.
15. It can keep you from getting hurt.
16. forgetting to close cabinet doors, riding in a car without wearing a seat belt
17. tell an adult or change the situation yourself

LESSON: SAFETY IN THE WATER

18. life jacket
19. Always go with an experienced person. Don't stand in the boat. Avoid boating in bad weather. Avoid rough water unless you know how to handle it.
20. Learn how to swim. Don't swim alone. Obey posted safety warnings. Swim in designated areas. Watch out for boats. Don't swim away from the shore. Avoid swimming in rough water and in bad weather.
21. you could hit your head or hurt your neck
22. swimming alone, improper diving, horseplay
23. Yell or call for help. Try to rescue the person from the shore or the side of the pool by using a pole or another long object. You could also throw a life preserver.
24. survival float

LESSON: WEATHER EMERGENCIES AND NATURAL DISASTERS

25. natural disaster
26. Emergency Alert System
27. a heavy rainstorm that has strong winds, lightning, and thunder
28. a spinning column of air that has high wind speeds and touches the ground
29. watch, warning
30. a large, spinning tropical weather system that has wind speeds of at least 74 miles per hour
31. flash flood
32. building damage, loss of water and electricity, landslides

LESSON: DEALING WITH EMERGENCIES

33. because if you give first aid incorrectly, you may hurt the victim more
34. 911

LESSON: GIVING FIRST AID

35. abdominal thrust
36. They cannot speak or breathe.
37. rescue breathing
38. Answers may vary. Sample answers: cleaning products, pesticides, car fluids
39. sterile gloves
40. A first-degree burn is red, mild, and not very deep. A second-degree burn is deeper, causes blisters, and is very painful. A third-degree burn is dark in color and deeper than second-degree burns.

Concept Mapping

LESSON: SAFETY AROUND HOME

Accidents include *falls*, fires, which can be avoided by having *smoke detectors* and *fire extinguishers*, and *electrocution*.

LESSON: WEATHER EMERGENCIES AND NATURAL DISASTERS

Answers may vary. Sample answer: *Natural disasters* include *floods*, *thunderstorms*, *earthquakes*, *hurricanes*, and *tornadoes*, during which your local *Emergency Alert System* issues *watches* and *warnings*.

Concept Review

LESSON: SAFETY AROUND HOME

1. Falls can be caused by tripping over objects or slipping on spills. Fires can be caused by open flame or overload power outlets. Electrocution can be caused by bare wires or lack of safety covers on outlets.
2. d
3. Wear safety gear. Pay attention to traffic, and avoid busy areas. Follow the rules of the road. Don't cycle or skate alone. Don't ride or skate after dark.
4. smoke detector
5. fire extinguisher

LESSON: SAFETY AT SCHOOL

6. anger, stress, illegal drugs, prejudice, negative peer pressure
7. violence
8. gang
9. If you don't feel safe at school, talk to your parents or school counselor. If you know about a violent situation, tell an adult. Brush up on your refusal skills, and learn conflict management skills. Find a positive way to spend your time.

LESSON: SEVEN WAY TO PROTECT YOURSELF

10. Think before you act—this can help you avoid injuries; pay attention—this can keep you from getting hurt; know your limits—this keeps you from hurting yourself and not putting something important to you at risk; practice refusal skills—using them in risky situations can keep you from getting hurt; use safety equipment—if you do have an accident, it can help you avoid injuries; change risky behavior—this can help prevent accidents; change risky situations—fixing or preventing them can help prevent accidents.
11. It keeps you floating in the water if there is an accident.
12. Learn how to swim. Don't swim alone. Obey posted safety warning. Swim in designated areas. Watch out for boats. Avoid swimming in rough water or in bad weather. Don't swim away from shore.
13. a
14. b
15. get in slowly, feet first
16. water survival float

LESSON: WEATHER EMERGENCIES AND NATURAL DISASTERS

17. e
18. c
19. d
20. a
21. f
22. b
23. Turn on the radio or TV to listen for EAS warnings. Listen for emergency sirens. Have a battery-operated radio in case the power goes out.

LESSON: DEALING WITH EMERGENCIES

24. first aid

25. You should give first aid to someone who is unconscious, not breathing, or in pain.
26. your name, your location, the type of emergency, the condition of the victim if someone is hurt, what you have done to care for a victim

LESSON: GIVING FIRST AID

27. Stand behind the victim. Place the thumb side of your fist against the victim's stomach. Your fist should be between the victim's belly button and breastbone. Cover your fist with your other hand. Quickly thrust inward and upward on the victim's stomach. Thrust five times in a row or until the object comes loose.
28. rescue breathing
29. Ask the victim what he or she ate. If the victim isn't awake, look for clues about the cause of poisoning. Call 911, and then call your local poison control center.
30. Wear sterile gloves. Cover the injury with gauze. Put pressure on the wound. Elevate the injured area.
31. A first-degree burn is red, mild, and not very deep. Second-degree burns are deeper than first-degree burns. They cause blisters and are very painful. Third-degree burns are dark in color and deeper than second-degree burns. These burns destroy pain receptors, so they usually aren't as painful as second-degree burns.

Refusal Skills

LESSON: SAFETY AT SCHOOL

Answers may vary. Sample answer: Dear Scared, Yes, you should definitely tell your parents or an adult at school. I know you don't want to get this person in trouble, but the situation could become dangerous. If he still insists, tell him "no" as firmly as you can and walk away. By refusing to go along with his plan you are protecting not only yourself but also other people. Sincerely, Know-It-All

LESSON: SEVEN WAYS TO PROTECT YOURSELF

Answers may vary. Sample answers:

1. I would tell my friend I don't want to jump in.
2. I could suggest another activity to cool us off, such as going home and spraying each other with the hose.
3. I could tell them how dangerous rivers can be.
4. I could leave the river.
5. I could avoid fishing by the river with people who practice risky behavior.
6. I have friends who do not think it is safe to swim in the river. They will stand by my decision not to jump in.

Decision-Making Skills

LESSON: SAFETY IN THE WATER

Answers may vary. Sample answers:

1. how I will help Marcus
2. My safety is important, but I also want to rescue my friend.
3. I could jump into the pool to save Marcus. I could throw him a life preserver.
4. If I jump into the pool, he could pull me under the water. If I throw him a life preserver, we will both be safe.
5. I will throw Marcus a life preserver and ask another swimmer to go find help.
6. I am happy with my decision because Marcus got out of the pool, and we were both safe. It was the correct action to take in the situation, and I'd do it again.

LESSON: DEALING WITH EMERGENCIES

Answers may vary. Sample answer: Bethany ran inside the house and called 911. She gave them her name and location. She told the operator that Timmy fell off the swing and was unconscious. After she gave all the information to the operator, she hung up and went outside to stay with Timmy until the ambulance arrived. They were able to wake Timmy on the way to the hospital, and he was fine. The medical workers congratulated Bethany for making the right decisions and staying calm.

Cross-Disciplinary: Language Arts

LESSON: WEATHER EMERGENCIES AND NATURAL DISASTERS

Answers may vary. Check to ensure the students included the proper procedures for dealing with the type of weather emergency they choose.

Cross-Disciplinary: Art

LESSON: GIVING FIRST AID

Answers may vary, but computer-generated posters should accurately describe and explain rescue breathing.

Quiz

LESSON: SAFETY AROUND HOME

1. d
2. c
3. b
4. a
5. b
6. c

LESSON: SAFETY AT SCHOOL

1. c
2. a
3. b
4. d
5. a

LESSON: SEVEN WAYS TO PROTECT YOURSELF

1. b
2. d
3. a
4. d
5. b
6. b

LESSON: SAFETY IN THE WATER

1. b
2. a
3. d
4. c
5. a
6. d

LESSON: WEATHER EMERGENCIES AND NATURAL DISASTERS

1. f
2. g
3. a
4. c
5. d
6. e
7. b
8. h
9. j
10. i

LESSON: DEALING WITH EMERGENCIES

1. d
2. c
3. d
4. a
5. b

LESSON: GIVING FIRST AID

1. a
2. c
3. d
4. a
5. d

Chapter Test

1. smoke detector
2. violence
3. first aid
4. rescue breathing
5. tornado
6. life jacket
7. c
8. b
9. c
10. d
11. a
12. b
13. a
14. d
15. Electricity passes through the body and can stop a person's heart. The victim might also stop breathing, and have burns and internal injuries.
16. Sample answer: People who can't control their anger may become violent. People who are stressed may take out the frustration on others. People who use illegal drugs may hurt people to

get more drugs. Prejudice can cause some people to dislike and try to hurt others. Negative peer pressure may cause people to become violent in order to fit in.

17. think before you act; pay attention; know your limits; practice refusal skills; use safety equipment; change risky behavior; change risky situations
18. Answers may vary. Sample answer: Wear a life jacket. Always go with an experienced person. Don't stand in the boat. Avoid boating in bad weather; Avoid rough water unless you know how to handle it.
19. Answers may vary. Sample answer: Call an ambulance. Use a wet, clean cloth or a wet cold compress on burned skin. Keep burned area as clean as possible. Do not open blisters. Keep victim comfortable until help arrives. Do not remove any clothing that is stuck to the burn.
20. Answers may vary. Sample answer: The potential accidents could come from a fall because of the spilled juice on the floor, a fire because of the overloaded power outlet, and electrocution because the electric can opener is sitting next to the sink which is full of water. Fixing these risky situations would involve the following: wipe up spilled juice, provide one or two more power outlets for the appliances, and drain the sink then move the electric can opener to a safer spot.
21. Answers may vary. Sample answer: First aid can increase the chances of making a full recovery because it helps to save someone's life until professional medical care is available.
22. Do not run cool water over the burn. Instead, apply a damp, sterile bandage. Also, do not open any blisters.
23. Keep the burned area as clean as possible, and keep the victim comfortable until help arrives.

Performance-Based Assessment

Answers may vary. Sample answers:

5. Tornado, because we have a lot of tornadoes in this area.
6. Lie down under my desk
7. It is important for everyone to know exactly what to do in case of an emergency.
8. my teacher

Datasheet for In-Text Activity

1. Answers may vary, but students are likely to note that falls are common while fires and electrocutions are less common.
2. Sample answers: I can make sure I put all my things away so that no one trips. I can help keep an eye on my younger siblings to make sure they don't get hurt.

Life Skills: Assessing Your Health

LESSON: SAFETY AROUND HOME

1. Answers may vary.
2. Answers may vary.
3. Answers may vary.
4. It sounds an alarm when it detects smoke.
5. Answers may vary. Sample answer: There might be a fire in another part of the house. If you only have one smoke detector, it might take longer for you to be alerted to a fire.
6. once a month

Life Skills: Coping

LESSON: DEALING WITH EMERGENCIES

1. Get out of the house.
2. Answers may vary. Sample answer: the neighbor's house
3. 911
4. my name, my address, information about the fire
5. only after the operator has gotten all the information needed

6. Answers may vary. Sample answer: I would have called to them and tried to get them to leave the house with me. If they were trapped, I would leave the house and call for help.

Enrichment Activities

LESSON: SAFETY AROUND HOME

Students should write at least three paragraphs to summarize their interview with the firefighter.

LESSON: SAFETY AT SCHOOL

Students should make a bar graph that presents the findings of their surveys.

LESSON: SEVEN WAYS TO PROTECT YOURSELF

Students should make two circle graphs that present the results of their surveys.

LESSON: SAFETY IN THE WATER

Students' advertisements should include clear instructions, be easy to read and understand, and be visually interesting.

LESSON: WEATHER EMERGENCIES AND NATURAL DISASTERS

Students' should make a bar graph to present the results of their research.

LESSON: DEALING WITH EMERGENCIES

Student's pamphlets should include information about how to deal with emergencies and should contain illustrations to demonstrate the information. Students could then show their pamphlets to younger children in their school.

LESSON: GIVING FIRST AID

Students should create an video that demonstrates giving abdominal thrusts. Remind students that they will only pretend to do this in their video.

Health Inventory

Answers may vary. This worksheet can be used to start a discussion on home safety.

Health Behavior Contract

Accept all reasonable answers.

At-Home Activity

Accept all reasonable diagrams.

TEST ITEM LISTING

Health and Your Safety

MULTIPLE CHOICE

1. Which is a type of accident that can occur around home?
   a. electrocution
   b. fall
   c. fire
   d. All of the above

   Answer: D   Difficulty: 1   Section: 1   Objective: 1

2. How can you prevent falls?
   a. Leave objects on the stairs.
   b. Use a chair to get items that are out of reach.
   c. Wipe up spills right away.
   d. All of the above

   Answer: D   Difficulty: 1   Section: 1   Objective: 1

3. What can you use to detect smoke from a fire?
   a. fire extinguisher
   b. smoke detector
   c. Emergency Alert Service
   d. None of the above

   Answer: B   Difficulty: 1   Section: 1   Objective: 1

4. What can you use to put out a fire?
   a. fire extinguisher
   b. smoke detector
   c. Emergency Alert Service
   d. None of the above

   Answer: A   Difficulty: 1   Section: 1   Objective: 1

5. How can you avoid electrocution?
   a. Touch bare electrical wires.
   b. Avoid putting too many plugs in an outlet.
   c. Do not put safety covers on outlets.
   d. Use the blow-dryer in the bathtub.

   Answer: B   Difficulty: 1   Section: 1   Objective: 1

6. How can you stay safe in a vehicle?
   a. Distract the driver.
   b. Lay down in the back seat.
   c. Wear your seat belt.
   d. None of the above

   Answer: C   Difficulty: 1   Section: 1   Objective: 3

7. Which of the following is a cause of violence at school?
   a. stress
   b. illegal drugs
   c. negative peer pressure
   d. All of the above

   Answer: D   Difficulty: 1   Section: 2   Objective: 1

8. If you overhear someone at school threatening violence, what should you NOT do?
   a. keep it to yourself
   b. tell a parent
   c. tell a school counselor
   d. All of the above

   Answer: A   Difficulty: 1   Section: 1   Objective: 2

9. Which of the folowing is NOT a good way to protect yourself?
   a. think before you act
   b. ignore your surroundings
   c. know your limits
   d. use safety equipment

   Answer: B   Difficulty: 1   Section: 3   Objective: 1

10. Which of the following is an example of safety equipment?
    a. helmet
    b. rubber gloves
    c. goggles
    d. All of the above

    Answer: D   Difficulty: 1   Section: 3   Objective: 2

11. Which of the following is a risky behavior?
    a. not wearing your seat belt
    b. wearing a helmet while cyling
    c. closing cabinet doors
    d. None of the above

    Answer: A Difficulty: 1 Section: 3 Objective: 2

12. What type of safety equipment should you wear when you go skating?
    a. helmet
    b. elbow pads
    c. knee pads
    d. All of the above

    Answer: D Difficulty: 1 Section: 3 Objective: 2

13. What should you do if someone you know has a risky behavior?
    a. ignore it
    b. talk to him or her about it
    c. try the risky behavior yourself
    d. None of the above

    Answer: B Difficulty: 1 Section: 3 Objective: 1

14. What should you do if you spot a risky situation?
    a. ignore it
    b. tell an adult
    c. fix it, even if you get hurt
    d. All of the above

    Answer: B Difficulty: 1 Section: 3 Objective: 1

15. How should you get into an unfamiliar body of water?
    a. dive head first
    b. lower yourself in feet first
    c. jump into the water
    d. None of the above

    Answer: B Difficulty: 1 Section: 4 Objective: 1

16. Which of the following is NOT a safe boating practice?
    a. standing in the boat
    b. going with an experienced person
    c. avoiding bad weather
    d. All of the above

    Answer: A Difficulty: 1 Section: 4 Objective: 1

17. Which of the following will keep you safe while swimming?
    a. Don't swim alone.
    b. Swim in designated areas.
    c. Watch out for boats.
    d. All of the above

    Answer: D Difficulty: 1 Section: 4 Objective: 2

18. What should you do to avoid drowning?
    a. swim alone
    b. horseplay
    c. swim in areas with a lifeguard on duty
    d. None of the above

    Answer: C Difficulty: 1 Section: 4 Objective: 4

19. What should you NOT do to help a person who is drowning?
    a. jump in the water
    b. throw a life preserver
    c. call for help
    d. All of the above

    Answer: A Difficulty: 1 Section: 4 Objective: 5

20. What should you do if you get too tired while swimming?
    a. don't panic
    b. use the water survival float
    c. yell and wave for help
    d. All of the above

    Answer: D Difficulty: 1 Section: 4 Objective: 6

21. When should you give first aid?
    a. when someone is unconscious
    b. when someone is not breathing
    c. when you have taken a first-aid class
    d. All of the above

    Answer: D Difficulty: 1 Section: 6 Objective: 1

22. When should you NOT give first aid?
    a. when someone is not breathing
    b. when someone is in pain
    c. if you are in danger
    d. All of the above
    Answer: C Difficulty: 1 Section: 6 Objective: 1

23. What information should you give the operator during an emergency phone call?
    a. your name
    b. your location
    c. the type of emergency
    d. All of the above
    Answer: D Difficulty: 1 Section: 6 Objective: 2

24. What should you NOT do during an emergency call?
    a. hang up right away
    b. tell the operator what you have done to treat the victim
    c. give your location
    d. All of the above
    Answer: A Difficulty: 1 Section: 6 Objective: 2

25. If you see a house on fire, what should you do?
    a. run inside to see if someone needs help
    b. call 911
    c. ignore it
    d. None of the above
    Answer: B Difficulty: 1 Section: 6 Objective: 2

26. What technique should you use to help a person who is choking?
    a. abdominal thrusts
    b. water survival float
    c. rescue breathing
    d. None of the above
    Answer: A Difficulty: 1 Section: 7 Objective: 1

27. What technique should you use if a person is not breathing?
    a. abdominal thrusts
    b. water survival float
    c. rescue breathing
    d. None of the above
    Answer: C Difficulty: 1 Section: 7 Objective: 2

28. Which of the following is the most serious type of burn?
    a. first-degree
    b. sunburn
    c. second-degree
    d. third-degree
    Answer: D Difficulty: 1 Section: 67 Objective: 5

29. How should you treat a first-degree burn?
    a. run cool water over the burn
    b. pour ice water over the burn
    c. call an ambulance
    d. All of the above
    Answer: A Difficulty: 1 Section: 7 Objective: 5

30. What household items can cause poisoning?
    a. pesticides
    b. cleaning products
    c. car fluids
    d. All of the above
    Answer: D Difficulty: 1 Section: 7 Objective: 3

31. What is the leading cause of death for children and tees?
    a. electrocution
    b. drowning
    c. vehicle accidents
    d. falls
    Answer: C Difficulty: 1 Section: 1 Objective: 3

32. During which type of natural disaster does the ground shake?
    a. thunderstorm
    b. earthquake
    c. hurricane
    d. flood
    Answer: B Difficulty: 1 Section: 5 Objective: 2

33. A large, spinning tropical weather system that has wind speeds of at least 74 miles per hour is called a(n)
    a. thunderstorm.
    b. earthquake.
    c. hurricane.
    d. flood.

    Answer: C   Difficulty: 1   Section: 5   Objective: 2

34. An overflowing of water into areas that are normally dry is called a(n)
    a. thunderstorm.
    b. earthquake.
    c. hurricane.
    d. flood.

    Answer: D   Difficulty: 1   Section: 5   Objective: 2

35. A heavy rainstorm with strong winds, lightning and thunder is called a(n)
    a. thunderstorm.
    b. earthquake.
    c. hurricane.
    d. flood.

    Answer: A   Difficulty: 1   Section: 5   Objective: 2

36. Which of the following causes of violence results from forming an opinion about other people because they are different?
    a. stress
    b. prejudice
    c. anger
    d. negative peer pressure

    Answer: B   Difficulty: 1   Section: 2   Objective: 1

37. Which is the least severe type of burn?
    a. first-degree
    b. third-degree
    c. second-degree
    d. chemical

    Answer: A   Difficulty: 1   Section: 7   Objective: 5

38. What technique is used to help someone who is choking?
    a. rescue breathing
    b. EAS
    c. water survival float
    d. abdominal thrusts

    Answer: D   Difficulty: 1   Section: 7   Objective: 1

39. What should you make to help your family get out of the house in case there is a fire?
    a. smoke detector
    b. fire extinguisher
    c. escape plan
    d. fall plan

    Answer: C   Difficulty: 1   Section: 1   Objective: 1

40. Keeping small appliances next to water can cause
    a. fires.
    b. vehicle accidents.
    c. falls.
    d. electrocution.

    Answer: D   Difficulty: 1   Section: 1   Objective: 1

41. What should you wear to keep from getting hurt during a vehicle accident?
    a. seat belt
    b. knee pads
    c. helmet
    d. goggles

    Answer: A   Difficulty: 1   Section: 1   Objective: 3

42. Who should NOT sit in the front seat of a vehicle?
    a. adults
    b. people under 12 years old
    c. people over 12 years old
    d. anyone under 18

    Answer: B   Difficulty: 1   Section: 1   Objective: 3

43. Which is an example of negative peer pressure that can lead to violence?
    a. stress
    b. prejudice
    c. anger
    d. gangs

    Answer: D   Difficulty: 1   Section: 5   Objective: 2

44. Which is a positive way to spend your time?
    a. practicing risky behaviors
    b. joining a sports team
    c. joining a gang
    d. vandalizing property

    Answer: B Difficulty: 1 Section: 5 Objective: 2

45. Which is a spinning column of air that has high wind speeds and touches the ground?
    a. tornado
    b. earthquake
    c. hurricane
    d. flood

    Answer: A Difficulty: 1 Section: 5 Objective: 2

46. Which is a flood that rises and falls with very little warning?
    a. small flood
    b. fast flood
    c. deep flood
    d. flash flood

    Answer: D Difficulty: 1 Section: 5 Objective: 2

COMPLETION

47. A ____________________ is a small, battery-operated alarm that detects smoke from a fire.
    Answer: smoke detector
    Difficulty: 1 Section: 1 Objective: 1

48. Using physical force to hurt someone or cause damage is called ____________________.
    Answer: violence Difficulty: 1 Section: 2 Objective: 2

49. Emergency medical care for someone who has been hurt or is sick is called ____________________.
    Answer: first aid Difficulty: 1 Section: 6 Objective: 1

50. An emergency technique in which a rescuer gives air to someone who is not breathing is called ____________________
    Answer: rescue breathing
    Difficulty: 1 Section: 7 Objective: 2

51. A ____________________ is a spinning column of air that has high wind speeds and touches the ground.
    Answer: tornado Difficulty: 1 Section: 5 Objective: 2

52. A ____________________ is a vest that keeps you floating in the water.
    Answer: life jacket Difficulty: 1 Section: 4 Objective: 1

53. A(n) ____________________ is an unexpected event that may lead to injury.
    Answer: accident Difficulty: 1 Section: 1 Objective: 1

54. A ____________________ is a device that releases chemicals to put out a fire.
    Answer: fire extinguisher
    Difficulty: 1 Section: 1 Objective: 1

55. A(n) ____________________ is the process of applying pressure to a choking person's stomach to force an object out of their throats.
    Answer: abdominal thrust
    Difficulty: 1 Section: 7 Objective: 1

56. Heavy rainstorms that have strong winds, lightning, and thunder are called ____________________.
    Answer: thunderstorms
    Difficulty: 1 Section: 5 Objective: 2

57. A ____________________ is a large, spinning tropical weather system that has wind speeds of at least 74 miles per hour.
    Answer: hurricane Difficulty: 1 Section: 5 Objective: 2

58. A ____________________ is an overflowing of water into areas that are normally dry.
Answer: flood Difficulty: 1 Section: 5 Objective: 2

59. A(n) ____________________ is a shaking of the Earth's surface caused by movement along a break in the Earth's crust.
Answer: earthquake Difficulty: 1 Section: 5 Objective: 2

SHORT ANSWER

60. Explain what happens when someone is electrocuted.
Answer:
Electricity passes through the body and can stop a person's heart. The victim might also stop breathing, and have burns and internal injuries.
Difficulty: 1 Section: 1 Objective: 1

61. Describe five causes of violence.
Answer:
People who can't control their anger may become violent. People who are stressed may take out the frustration on others. People who use illegal drugs may hurt people to get more drugs. Prejudice can cause some people to dislike and try to hurt others. Negative peer pressure may cause people to become violent in order to fit in.
Difficulty: 1 Section: 2 Objective: 1

62. List seven ways to protect yourself from accidental injury.
Answer:
Think before you act; pay attention; know your limits; practice refusal skills; use safety equipment; change risky behavior; change risky situations
Difficulty: 1 Section: 3 Objective: 1

63. List five tips for boating safely.
Answer:
Wear a life jacket. Always go with an experienced person. Don't stand in the boat. Avoid boating in bad weather. Avoid rough water unless you know how to handle it.
Difficulty: 1 Section: 4 Objective: 1

64. Explain how to treat a third-degree burn.
Answer:
Call an ambulance. Use a wet, clean cloth or a wet cold compress on burned skin. Keep burned area as clean as possible. Do not open blisters. Keep victim comfortable until help arrives. Do not remove any clothing that is stuck to the burn.
Difficulty: 1 Section: 7 Objective: 5

65. Why should you wear a helmet when you ride a bicycle?
Answer: A helmet reduces your chances of a head injury.
Difficulty: 1 Section: 1 Objective: 2

66. What is electrocution?
Answer:
Electrocution is an accident in which electricity passes through a person's body.
Difficulty: 1 Section: 1 Objective: 1

67. Why should you wipe up water that you spilled on the floor?
Answer: People can slip on a wet floor and fall.
Difficulty: 1 Section: 1 Objective: 1

68. Name four things that could cause a fire.
    Answer:
    Open flame, frayed electrical cords, overloaded power outlets, and some chemicals
    Difficulty: 1 Section: 1 Objective: 1

69. What is violence?
    Answer: Violence is the use of physical force to hurt someone or cause damage.
    Difficulty: 1 Section: 2 Objective: 1

70. How can stress result in violence?
    Answer:
    Stress causes frustration. Some people take out their frustration on other people.
    Difficulty: 1 Section: 2 Objective: 1

71. How can illegal drugs lead to violence?
    Answer:
    Drugs cause people to act differently. Some people want drugs so much that they are willing to hurt other people to get drugs.
    Difficulty: 1 Section: 2 Objective: 1

72 How does joining a sports team or school club help you avoid violence?
    Answer:
    These activities keep you out of violent situations and are a positive way to spend your time.
    Difficulty: 1 Section: 2 Objective: 2

73. Why is it important to pay attention to your surroundings to stay safe?
    Answer:
    When you pay attention, you know about accidents that could happen and you can avoid them.
    Difficulty: 1 Section: 3 Objective: 2

74. How can you practice your refusal skills?
    Answer:
    Sample answer: You can practice with your parents and friends. You can think of situations that are hard to refuse and come up with ways to say no.
    Difficulty: 2 Section: 3 Objective: 2

75. What are three examples of safety equipment?
    Answer: Sample answer: rubber gloves, goggles, and helmets
    Difficulty: 1 Section: 3 Objective: 2

76. Which of the following is a risky behavior: reading a book, riding your bike down the block with no helmet, or dying your hair purple?
    Answer: riding your bike down the block without a helmet
    Difficulty: 1 Section: 3 Objective: 2

77. Why do many swimming areas post safety warnings?
    Answer:
    Sample answer: Signs around swimming areas let you know about safety risks.
    Difficulty: 1 Section: 4 Objective: 2

78. Why shouldn't you dive head first into an unknown body of water?
    Answer:
    Sample answer: If you aren't familiar with a body of water, you don't know how deep it is. If you dive head first into shallow water, you could hurt your head or neck.
    Difficulty: 2 Section: 4 Objective: 3

79. Why should you swim in areas with a lifeguard?
    Answer:
    Sample answer: Lifeguards are trained to save you if you have an accident in or near the water.
    Difficulty: 1 Section: 4 Objective: 4

80. Why shouldn't you stand up in a boat?
    Answer: Sample answer: The boat might tip over, or you may fall out of it.
    Difficulty: 2 Section: 4 Objective: 1

81. What is a natural disaster?
    Answer:
    A natural disaster is a natural event that causes widespread injury, death, and property damage.
    Difficulty: 1 Section: 5 Objective: 2

82. What is the EAS and what does it do?
    Answer:
    Sample answer: The EAS is the Emergency Alert System. During a storm or emergency, the EAS sends a tone and special instructions through the TV or radio.
    Difficulty: 2 Section: 5 Objective: 1

83. What is a flash flood?
    Answer: A flash flood is a flood that rises and falls with very little warning.
    Difficulty: 1 Section: 5 Objective: 2

84. If you are outside when an earthquake occurs, what should you do?
    Answer:
    Sample answer: Avoid buildings, power lines, and trees. Find an open area. Lie down, and cover you head.
    Difficulty: 2 Section: 5 Objective: 2

85. Name three things you should look for when you find someone who has been hurt.
    Answer:
    Sample answer: I should check to see if the victim is conscious, look for obvious injuries, and see if the victim is breathing.
    Difficulty: 2 Section: 6 Objective: 1

86. Why should you check the area around a victim first?
    Answer:
    Sample answer: I need to make sure I'm safe. Whatever hurt the victim could also hurt me.
    Difficulty: 2 Section: 6 Objective: 1

87. What phone numbers should be included in an emergency telephone list?
    Answer:
    911, the police department, the fire department, the poison control center, your parents at work, your doctor, your neighbors, and other family members
    Difficulty: 1 Section: 6 Objective: 2

88. Your friend is eating a peanut-butter-and-jelly sandwich. Suddenly, she begins to choke. She is unable to cough or speak and looks scared. What should you do?
    Answer: Sample answer: I should call for help and give her abdominal thrusts.
    Difficulty: 2 Section: 7 Objective: 1

89. What is rescue breathing?
    Answer:
    Rescue breathing is an emergency technique in which a rescuer gives air to someone who is not breathing.
    Difficulty: 1 Section: 7 Objective: 2

90. Which type of burn may not be very painful? Why?
    Answer:
    Sample answer: Third-degree burns may not be very painful because pain receptors have been destroyed.
    Difficulty: 2 Section: 7 Objective: 5

91. Explain what it means to know your limits.
    Answer:
    Sample answer: You should know your physical limits and don't do an activity you know you aren't ready to do. You also have limits based on your values. If something is important to you, you probably won't do anything to put it at risk.
    Difficulty: 2 Section: 3 Objective: 2

92. What can you do if you know someone who has risky behavior?
    Answer: I can let him or her know about it, and then we can work on changing it.
    Difficulty: 1 Section: 3 Objective: 2

93. Who should you tell if you see a risky situation in your home?
    Answer: my parents Difficulty: 1 Section: 3 Objective: 3

94. What is the difference between a watch and a warning?
    Answer:
    A watch lets people know that a tornado may happen. A warning lets people know that a tornado has been spotted.
    Difficulty: 1 Section: 5 Objective: 1

95. If you are inside during a tornado, where should you go?
    Answer:
    into the basement or cellar, or to a windowless room in the center of the building
    Difficulty: 1 Section: 5 Objective: 2

96. What is the best thing to do during a flood?
    Answer: Find a high place to wait out the flood.
    Difficulty: 1 Section: 5 Objective: 2

ESSAY

97. Steve walked into his kitchen. The sink was fullof water, and the electric can opener was sitting next to the sink. The can opener, microwave, toaster, blender, and mixer are all plugged into the same outlet. There is some juice spilled on the floor. Help Steve identify the potential accidents in the kitchen. Then, identify how to fix these risky situations.
    Answer:
    The potential accidents could come from a fall because of the spilled juice on the floor, a fire because of the overloaded power outlet, and electrocution because the electric can opener is sitting next to the sink which is full of water. Fixing these risky situations would involve the following: wipe up the spilled juice, provide one or two more power outlets for the appliances, and drain the sink then move the electric can opener to a safer spot.
    Difficulty: 2 Section: 7 Objective: 1

98. Marlene notices her two year old sister, Denise, has stopped breathing. Her parents are not around. Marlene has taken a first-aid class. Describe the steps Marlene should take to help Denise.

    Answer:

    Marlene should call for help. Then she should lay Denise on her back and open her airway by tilting her head back and lifting her chin. Marlene should look, listen, and feel for breathing. If Denise is not breathing, Marlene should put her mouth over Denise's nose and mouth and give her small, fast breaths. Marlene should make sure the chest is rising and continue rescue breathing until Denise starts breathing again or help arrives.

    Difficulty: 2 Section: 7 Objective: 2

Examine the diagram below, and answer the questions that follow.

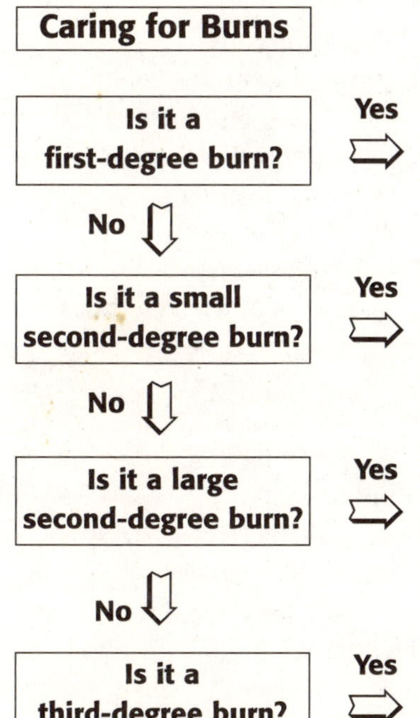

Yes ⇨ Run cool water over the burn, or use a cold compress on the burn, until the pain goes away. Do not use ice or ice water on the burn. Use antibiotic cream on the burn while it heals. If the burn is very large or on the face, call a doctor.

Yes ⇨ Use a damp, sterile bandage or a wet cold compress on the burned area of skin. Do not open blisters. Use antibiotic cream on the burn while it heals. If the burn is on the face, call a doctor.

Yes ⇨ Hold a clean, damp cloth or a wet cold compress on the burned areas. Do not open blisters. Call an ambulance, or ask an adult to take the victim to the Emergency Room. Do not remove any clothing that is stuck to the burn.

Yes ⇨ Call an ambulance. Use a wet, clean cloth or a wet cold compress on burned skin. Keep burned area as clean as possible. Do not open blisters. Keep victim comfortable until help arrives. Do not remove any clothing that is stuck to the burn.

99. Explain how you would treat a small second-degree burn differently than you would treat a first-degree burn.

    Answer:

    Use a damp, sterile bandage on the burned ara, and do not open any blister.s

    Difficulty: 2 Section: 7 Objective: 5

100. Explain how you would treat a third-degree burn differently than you would treat a large second-degree burn.

    Answer:

    Keep the burned areas as clean as possible, and keep the victim comfortable until help arrives.

    Difficulty: 2 Section: 7 Objective: 5

MATCHING

a. natural disaster
b. thunderstorm
c. tornado
d. hurricane
e. flood
f. earthquake
g. EAS
h. thunder
i. watch
j. warning
k. violence
l. gang
m. prejudice
n. smoke detector
o. fire extinguisher
q. abdominal thrusts
r. rescue breathing

101.____ shaking of the Earth's surface caused by movement along a break in the Earth's crust
Answer: F Difficulty: 1 Section: 5 Objective: 2

102.____ system used by radio and TV stations to warn people of a weather emergency
Answer: G Difficulty: 1 Section: 5 Objective: 1

103.____ natural event that causes widespread injury, death, and property damage
Answer: A Difficulty: 1 Section: 5 Objective: 2

104.____ spinning column of air that has high wind speeds and touches the ground
Answer: C Difficulty: 1 Section: 5 Objective: 2

105.____ large, spinning tropical weather system that has wind speeds of at least 74 miles per hour
Answer: D Difficulty: 1 Section: 5 Objective: 2

106.____ overflowing of water into areas that are normally dry
Answer: E Difficulty: 1 Section: 5 Objective: 2

107.____ heavy rainstorm with strong winds, lightning, and thunder
Answer: B Difficulty: 1 Section: 5 Objective: 2

108.____ sound waves created when air expands
Answer: H Difficulty: 1 Section: 5 Objective: 2

109.____ weather alert that lets people know a tornado has been spotted
Answer: J Difficulty: 1 Section: 5 Objective: 2

110.____ weather alert that lets people know that a tornado may happen
Answer: I Difficulty: I Section: 5 Objective: 1

111.____ forming an opinion about other people because they are different
Answer: M Difficulty: 1 Section: 1 Objective: 1

112.____ using physical force to hurt someone or cause damage
Answer: K Difficulty: 1 Section: 1 Objective: 1

113.____ group of people who often use violence
Answer: L Difficulty: 1 Section: 1 Objective: 1

114.____ releases chemicals to put out a fire
Answer: O Difficulty: 1 Section: 7 Objective: 1

115.____ giving air to someone who is not breathing
Answer: R Difficulty: 1 Section: 7 Objective: 2

116.____ used to help someone who is choking
Answer: Q Difficulty: 1 Section: 2 Objective: 1

117.____ detects smoke from a fire
Answer: N Difficulty: 1 Section: 1 Objective: 1

9997256530 1 2 3 4 5 6